EXPLAINING
New Testament Baptism

DAVID PAWSON

ANCHOR RECORDINGS

Copyright © 2016 David Pawson

The right of David Pawson to be identified as author of this Work has been asserted by him in accordance with the Copyright, Designs and Patents Act 1988.

First published in Great Britain in 2016 by
Anchor Recordings Ltd
Synegis House, 21 Crockhamwell Road,
Woodley, Reading RG5 3LE

No part of this publication may be reproduced or transmitted in any form or by any means, electronic or mechanical, including photocopy, recording or any information storage and retrieval system, without prior permission in writing from the publisher.

**For more of David Pawson's teaching,
including DVDs and CDs, go to
www.davidpawson.com**

FOR FREE DOWNLOADS
www.davidpawson.org

**For further information,
email: info@davidpawsonministry.com**

ISBN 978-1-911173-33-5

Printed by Lightning Source

This booklet is based on a talk. Originating as it does from the spoken word, its style will be found by many readers to be somewhat different from my usual written style. It is hoped that this will not detract from the substance of the biblical teaching found here.

As always, I ask the reader to compare everything I say or write with what is written in the Bible and, if at any point a conflict is found, always to rely upon the clear teaching of scripture.

David Pawson

EXPLAINING
New Testament Baptism

THE FIRST INTERVIEW
Interviewer: *Mr Pawson, you are most welcome to Finland. It is so wonderful to have you here again. You came here originally to attend a debate about baptism. I think many viewers would want to hear more of your view on baptism since it is a hot debate – and a hot discussion right now here in Finland. But first of all, I want to ask you: were you yourself baptised as a baby?*

David: Yes, I was – I have a certificate to prove it. But that's all I remember about it. I was baptised by my grandfather. I was born into a family that was very prominent in one of our largest denominations in England, the Methodist Church, and they of course baptise babies. So I was baptised and since my grandfather was the minister/pastor, he baptised me. Then, many years later, after I had gone into farming (I was hoping to be a farmer), the Lord called me into full-time service of the church. Since I only knew one denomination, the Methodist Church, I offered to them and they accepted me. So, after training, I found myself baptising babies, so I was on that side of the fence for most of my early life.

Interviewer: *Well, I understand you've changed your view since. What made you change your mind?*

David: It's quite a story. It all happened in Arabia. The Methodist church decided that I should be a chaplain in the Royal Air Force. That's someone who is a pastor in the forces and looks after the souls of the airmen, and they sent me out to Aden. And my parish stretched from there, right up the Persian Gulf, to Bahrain and most of Arabia, and it was there that three things happened. First, I got married. And, you know, the first time I met my wife she came to ask me about baptism. She had been baptised as a baby and her sister had become a Baptist and was now a Baptist missionary out in Africa, in Angola, and this had troubled her. It made her think about her baptism, and so she came to ask me for advice and I had to say, 'Well, I've got my questions too.' That is how we met and fell in love – over baptism – and she was the first person I baptised as a believer.

But that is jumping ahead. We had our first child soon out in Arabia and therefore we had to face the question: What are we going to do about our children? Will we have them baptised like we were, or what shall we do? It made me think about it in a much more realistic way – when it is your own child and not somebody else's, it becomes a little more personal. That was the first thing.

The second thing that happened to me was that I discovered that any Muslim who became a believer in Christ in Arabia was murdered. They weren't murdered when they said they became a Christian or when they went to church or when they carried a Bible around. They were – every one – murdered *when they were baptised*. I thought: what is it about baptism the Muslims take so seriously? And I discovered they had a much deeper understanding of baptism than I had. They really saw it as a burial of the past, as the end of an old life. So therefore the person who was baptised was now a traitor to Islam and that of course deserves death.

Then the third thing happened. I wasn't getting very

far with preaching to airmen – to men. I was used to congregations of women and children, and I thought: what can I do to get these men really interested? I felt the Lord tell me: 'Teach them the Bible.'

I said, 'But I do that.'

He answered: 'No, you don't. You teach them texts – verses of the Bible, bits of the Bible. I want you to teach them the whole Bible.'

So I said, 'I'll take you through the whole Bible from "Generation" to "Revolution" in just three months.' And I did. You know, it fired up those men and they really came alive. They saw the whole picture and not just little bits. Therefore, because I was asking questions about baptism, I began to study every bit of the Bible about baptism.

There is nothing in the Old Testament, so that was easy, but the New Testament has thirty-one separate passages all about baptism, and when I began to put these passages together and get a whole picture, I really had a bit of a shock. I thought: I don't understand baptism at all! I had done it, I had accepted the tradition of the church without question, and I was even practising the tradition of the church without question. But now I really had problems, and I'm afraid I then came to the conclusion that I had been wrong and that I couldn't practise infant baptism any more – not with my own children, not with anybody else's.

Interviewer: *So I assume that you were baptised then.*

David: Eventually, yes. Because I had to ask, 'Am I baptised?' Now I was baptised in the sight of the church but I was asking now: But am I baptised in the sight of the Lord?

Interviewer: *Good question!*

David: Can I apply these thirty-one passages to my baptism as a baby? I couldn't do it, so I had to face the question. I wasn't baptised *again*, because I don't think baptism can ever be repeated. It is a one-off in the life of every Christian. Really, I had to come to the conclusion that my baptism as a baby was not a New Testament baptism and therefore, though everybody else said, 'You're getting baptised again,' I said, 'No, I'm not, I'm getting baptised for the first time.' I want to make that point very strongly, because anybody who wants to be baptised as a believer after being baptised as a baby has to come to the conclusion that it is not a re-baptism or a second baptism, but that the first was not valid and therefore the second is the first real baptism.

Interviewer: *Well there, quite a change – quite a process for a man who was a Methodist minister! So what did it mean to you, these conclusions that you arrived to?*

David: Well, it created a crisis. Can I talk about my baptism first, what it meant to me?

Interviewer: *Sure.*

David: It was in a little Baptist church up in the Pennine Hills in the North of England. A friend of mine said he would do it and so I went – not knowing what to expect or what it would mean, but knowing that my *baby* baptism meant nothing – I couldn't remember it; didn't think about it. What would this mean? Well, it was an old, church and it had a baptistry, a pool which hadn't been used I think for a long, long time because it was green with mould. As I went down into the water, down the steps, and saw this green, I had a vision and I saw only the Jordan river, and the Jordan valley with a green bank either side, and I sensed Jesus had just gone down into the river in front of me, and that I was next. It was an extraordinary vision and I felt, 'I'm following Jesus.' And of course he was baptised at the age of 30 when he went down into the Jordan and I really had this extraordinary sense that I wasn't in the church at all, and that I was in the Jordan River and that I was following Jesus and doing what he did. It was a simple experience but it was visual, and it must have been sparked off by this green mould on the side of the pool, but it was very meaningful to me.

But of course, yes, it raised a crisis. Here I am, the minister of a church expected to be baptising babies, having promised to do so when I was ordained, and said I would minister the Word and sacraments according to the use of the Methodist Church. That was the vow I had taken.

Interviewer: *What did it mean for your ministry then?*

David: Well, I had to tell the authorities of the Methodist church: I can no longer baptise babies. So they brought me before a disciplinary committee. It was rather amusing because on the committee was a professor who had written a book supporting believers' baptism, even though he was a Methodist professor! And the chairman asked me, What have you been reading that has changed your mind? Well, I said, 'For one thing, I have read this professor's book, and this caused consternation. The professor blushed. But eventually they felt they couldn't do anything, that they couldn't kick me out and so they didn't. They didn't say, 'You can't go on,' they said, 'Well, we'll give you a church,' and that was it – except that they said, 'We'll give you an assistant to do all the baptisms for you, and then your conscience will be happy.' I said, 'No, that would be dishonest. That's hard on the assistant and in any case I will now be preaching about baptism in a different way, and there would be a conflict within the church. I'm afraid I must resign.'

They were glad that I had taken the initiative. I said to my wife when I went home, 'We're going to lose my job, my pension and our house, and I have nothing else to offer you.'

I will never forget what she said: 'David, I want to be married to a man who obeys God.'

So that was that. And do you know, within one week we had a brand new house that nobody had lived in, and I was the pastor of a Baptist church. It really is an amazing story. I found out then that my employer was not the church but the Lord and that really he was paying me and he would find me a job. So I have been working for him ever since.

Interviewer: *You mentioned that after a week you had joined the Baptist Church. How did all that happen? How did you join them?*

David: When I realised that I could not conscientiously go on being a Methodist minister, I had to say, 'Which other church do I join?' And my question was: which of all the churches in England is preaching and practising New Testament baptism as I now understand it? And none of them were.

Interviewer: *None of them?*

David: None of them! It was extraordinary. I'll tell you in a moment. They all fell into two groups. Each was practising about half of the New Testament teaching on baptism but not the rest – a different half. The only denomination that I could find was in America and it's called the Churches of Christ or the Disciples of Christ. Now they have a few, tiny little branches in England but nothing really, so there was nothing to join in England. So I looked around and I said, 'Well, the Baptists at least *practise* New Testament baptism in the way that I've come to believe in it. They may not *preach* it but then the advantage of the Baptist churches was that each church is independent and autonomous. They are not under an authority, a central headquarters. They are each free to pursue the way the Lord leads them.' So I thought: I will be free to practise New Testament baptism and, in that church, free to preach it as well, because they don't impose doctrinal standards from the top.

So, since the Baptist churches were a major denomination in Britain and they were happy to have me, that was it. They accredited me and I began my ministry as a Baptist pastor. When I am asked today what I am, I say, 'I'm a Methibaptican, because the Methodist Church ordained me, the Baptist Church accredited me, and two Anglican Bishops asked if they could lay hands on me for my ministry!'

But I minister in everything from Pentecostal to Roman Catholic and everything in between.

Interviewer: *That's right. You mention the term 'New Testament baptism' a lot. So what does that mean to you?*

David: As quickly as I can: first of all, it certainly means *baptism by immersion*. The very Greek word 'baptizein' means to put a solid into a liquid. It is used of dipping a glass into a bowl of wine; it is used of a ship being sunk (not a ship being launched, but a ship being sunk – then it is 'baptised'); or it is used of dyeing wool and you put the wool right in the dye – that is baptising. So the first simple conclusion I came to is that baptism is by immersion. And it is interesting that even all the Orthodox Churches baptise babies by immersion. They know the meaning of the Greek word. It never meant sprinkling or moistening. In fact, the New Testament says clearly John the Baptist baptised at a place called Aenon near Salim 'because there was much water there'. And every baptism in the New Testament talks about someone going down into the water and coming up out of the water. So that was the first very simple conclusion.

But then I tackled a much more important question – not *how* should we baptise according to the New Testament but *why*, and it was then that I discovered that baptism in essence is a joint action between God and man – that God does things in baptism but that man should also do things for baptism. And what I found was that most churches divide into these two groups: those who only see what God does in baptism and see nothing needed on the part of the human side, therefore a baby can be baptised. The baby does nothing; God does everything. Then there were, on the other hand, Pentecostals and Baptists, and many of them put all the emphasis on what man does in baptism – that he's obeying the Lord; that he's testifying to others, a kind of 'wet witness'. I never heard any Baptist talk about what God does in baptism.

Interviewer: *I heard this term, that baptism is an 'act of obedience'. I've heard this term used a lot.*

David: Well of course it is. But it is much more than that. And so here were these two groups, those who baptised babies and said, 'God does all this', and those who baptise believers as more or less adults who were either obeying or testifying or witnessing. Nobody was bringing those two sides together and that's what I found.

Let us just summarise what God does in the New Testament. The New Testament links baptism with washing sins away, with forgiveness, with being saved, with being born again ('born of water and the Spirit'), all of which *God* does. But then I noticed in the New Testament that man needs to do something as well or it isn't New Testament baptism, and I found that four things always had to happen before a baptism was valid, before someone was eligible or qualified. First, they needed to hear the gospel. That's the very first thing. They needed to hear the good news about Jesus. Second, they needed to believe that good news; to believe the very minimum of three things: that Jesus is the Son of God, that he died for our sins, and that he was raised again from the dead on the third day. So first to hear that; second to believe it. Thirdly, to repent of their sins, to realise that they were on the wrong side of God, and really to think again and to confess them, and to turn their back on them – turn away from them. Repentance is in thought, word and deed. It is a really amazing thing to do. And the fourth thing was to call on the name of Jesus themselves.

You know when Ananias the old man came to Saul of Tarsus after he'd met the Lord on the Damascus road and been blinded, of course, by the light of the glory of the

Lord. Ananias said, 'What are you waiting for? Get up and be baptised and have your sins washed away, calling on his name.' Now when I looked at those things, that all came *before* baptism in the New Testament, not after. It was always, 'Repent and be baptised....' 'He who believes and is baptised shall be saved.' It was always that order. The human action came first and then God acted in response to that, never the other way round. And I simply had to say, Can a baby do those four things? Can a baby hear the gospel? Can a baby understand and believe it? Can a baby repent? I have never yet met anybody who baptised babies who claimed that babies can repent. And do you know, even if they could, what would they repent of? Babies haven't sinned yet. And, fourthly, calling on his name – and I never heard a baby doing that.

So quite simply – it is so simple – it seemed utterly logical that New Testament baptism was not to babies and that human action needed to happen first, and then someone could be baptised. Then God would do these amazing things in baptism for that person.

Interviewer: *I want to take hold of one point. I hear many times emphasised that it is a work of grace that comes from God – baptism is a gift of grace from God and God does everything. As you said, that's one of the views. But you said that there are some certain elements that we need to do before we are baptised. But isn't that teaching salvation by works? I'm sure many people would think like this.*

David: Well, what do we mean by works? If we mean 'good deeds', no way! I didn't list that. If we mean actions on our part, yes! You see, the problem is this word 'works'. People really misuse that. In fact, my New Testament says, 'Faith without works is dead. It cannot save.' That's James 2, which Martin Luther hated. He said it was a right straw epistle. But it is part of the Word of God. I would translate that: 'Faith without action is dead. It cannot save.' Faith is an active thing that we *do*. Repentance is an *active* thing that we do. Call them works if you like, but to say that is salvation by works is a complete distortion.

You see, the classical text for salvation is, 'By grace are we saved through faith.' Grace is what God does and faith is what we do, and both are essential. Now we're not saved by our faith. We're not saved by what we do. We're saved *through* what we do. In other words, we can't be saved without that. You can't be saved by grace without faith, and faith is our part and grace is his part. And when we believe, grace saves. God is always responding to us and he wants us to take those steps.

To take another issue, which I've already mentioned, God cannot forgive a person who doesn't repent first. That's the teaching of scripture. We can't forgive each other unless someone's repented. Jesus said, 'If your brother sins against you seven times a day, forgive him seven times a day, if he repents.' Now most people have never noticed that little phrase. God can't forgive me if I don't repent. He expects me to say, 'I have sinned, I'm stopping that, I'm turning away from that, I'm renouncing it. If it's something that I can put right, I'll put it right.' All that is repentance – and God forgives when we repent. So repenting and believing are what we do to make it possible for grace to save us. Now call that salvation by works and I think that's a complete misunderstanding. Never are repentance or faith called 'works' in the New Testament. They are *actions*, and they are actions that we do but they don't deserve salvation and they don't give salvation but they make it possible for God to show his grace towards us.

But so many people will say, 'Oh no, grace operates first' – the other way round. My New Testament doesn't say that. It says grace is available for everybody but unless we repent and believe, that grace is useless.

Interviewer: *So let's talk about infant baptism then. Why do you think many churches do this practice?*

David: One simple answer is: because it has nearly always been done. It has been done for a very long time. It is a long historical tradition. It doesn't go back to the New Testament but it goes back a long way and it has been passed on from one generation to another, within the church and even within families. Often it is grandparents who want the baby 'done' rather than the parents, but nevertheless, it is something that's been passed down. And when we ask why it has been done, different reasons are given. It used to be believed that the baby would go to hell if it wasn't baptised. That is a wicked belief. But then it was softened a bit in the Middle Ages by teaching that babies unbaptised wouldn't go to hell, they would go to another place which wasn't quite as bad, called *limbus infantum* to give it its Latin name, or 'limbo'. And so unbaptised babies used to go to limbo.

Now parents who feared for their babies rushed to get them baptised of course. When that is taught, that really puts fear of hell into parents. It has been softened a bit further than that, and in the Methodist Church they did it because they said it's to show that God loves the baby before the baby loves God. And that's a truth, but in my New Testament baptism wasn't intended to convey that truth. That's the justification I was brought up on, that it is to show that God wants every baby to be his. But to me that is not a sufficient reason and it is not even a New Testament reason for baptising a baby.

So, it has been a long tradition. There have been people all the way through church history who read their Bible and who practised believers' baptism but they were often very small groups and persecuted by the big church.

Interviewer: *So you are saying it was not just a new invention in the 1500s, at the time of the Reformation, and* *that alongside Luther and the other Reformers suddenly these Anabaptists appeared somewhere, but it has always been there as a part of church history?*

David: Both Luther and Calvin kept up the tradition of the Roman church in baptising babies, but because Luther had released the Bible and translated it into German so people could read it, more and more people were reading the Bible, and because of that, a whole group of people reading the Bible restored New Testament baptism. They were naughtily called by the main churches 'Anabaptists' and '*ana*' means 'twice' or 'again'. So they were called the 'twice baptisers', or the 'again baptisers', which was very naughty because they were convinced that they were baptising for the first time. But there it was. And they were persecuted. I am afraid they were persecuted by the Protestant reforming churches and subject to a terrible punishment. They were drowned. I have stood in Zurich in Switzerland at the edge of the river there where Baptists were drowned because they were questioning the practice of baby baptism. It was one of the sad features of the Protestant Reformation. Here were Protestants drowning Protestants, which is an extraordinary business. So when Catholics had persecuted Protestants, now Protestants were persecuting their own.

But all that is history. To me, scripture is a greater authority for me than history. And it was for Martin Luther. Martin Luther himself, when he discovered the Bible – really discovered it – began to question so many traditions in the church of very long standing. And when he was brought to trial for the radical reformation that he was doing, he said, 'My conscience is captive to the Word of God. Here I stand. I can do no other.' Then he was kidnapped – and, for his own safety, hidden away in a castle. But I stand with Luther there. My conscience is captive to the Word of God and even if babies have been baptised for 1800 years, I still say what the Bible says is what I must go by. And it was my study of the Bible that changed my mind.

Interviewer: *So why do you think that Luther originally kept the practice of baptising babies?*

David: It's a complicated question to answer, but I think the simplest thing to say is that it was because he kept the concept of the State Church. The church and State for centuries had been interlocked in what was called 'The Holy Roman Empire', and Martin Luther's Reformation was essentially achieved by State power when he persuaded a State to become Protestant. And Germany was made up of many states – Saxony and all their little states – and when the head of a state became Protestant, the whole state had to, and therefore citizenship in the state and membership in the church were almost one and the same thing. You were born into both, and frankly, you can't have a State Church that baptises believers. It is a contradiction. If a State Church ever said, 'We are only going to baptise those who believe in Jesus,' it will cease to be the State Church, because everybody won't bring their babies to be baptised, and therefore baby baptism and State Churches go together and Luther never reformed the State Church into a free church. Now, what is going to happen in the 21st Century? State Churches are going to die anyway. They are on the way out everywhere.

Interviewer: *That's a bold statement.*

David: Yes, but they're going to be replaced. Some of the churches in the State Church will survive and grow but they will be free churches as all the other free churches are. So that doesn't mean all the State Churches will go, but those that survive will be more free churches – will not depend on the State for financial support or anything else.

Interviewer: *Why do you say this? Where do you base this idea that they're on their way out?*

David: On sheer statistics. The Church of England is losing 1000 people a week. It is a State Church. There are some Anglican churches that are really thriving, but the overall picture is it's on the way out. It's free churches that are growing, churches that are independent of the State and have to find their own resources.

Interviewer: *We don't have much time left but I would still want to ask: Can the baptism of babies be supported by scripture in your opinion?*

David: We're going to have another talk aren't we? I think I'd rather leave that one till the next talk because that would take quite a lot of time.

Interviewer: *That's right. Well, do you think that it's wrong to baptise babies? In your opinion.*

David: Yes. That is my simple answer. I think it is damaging. Can I start with a statistic, because one fact is worth a lot of opinion. Here in Finland, over 90% of the people have been baptised as babies. Less than 3% are in church. What has gone wrong? To put it very crudely, it doesn't seem to have taken; it doesn't seem to have worked. It is robbing people of the experience and memory of baptism, which means such a lot to people who have been baptised and know it, who have voluntarily and consciously been immersed in the name of Jesus. You never forget it. It is robbing thousands of people of that experience. It is saying: you can't have that now because somebody else decided for you when you were a baby, and so you can't have this now – and this causes immense tension in so many people.

But the biggest damage it does is to tell people something that is not true. It is saying you are a Christian because you were christened as a baby. You have been saved; you are forgiven; you belong to Christ – when in fact they do not. And that is a false security that sooner or later will be shown up.

Interviewer: *These things that you are telling us are most interesting but unfortunately we are running out of time, so we have to finish it here. But, gladly, we have another programme coming on the same subject so we can pick it up right where we left it this time. Thank you so much for your teaching Mr Pawson. We are so glad to have you here. Thank you.*

THE SECOND INTERVIEW

Interviewer: *Hello Mr Pawson, you are most welcome to our second programme on baptism. We are so glad to have you here a second time to discuss this very vital subject. Last time, we looked at your personal history and the fact that you had been baptised as a baby but then you came to change your mind, and we also talked about the New Testament requirements of baptism, and then we touched on a little bit of the history of infant baptism. Now I would like to jump directly into that subject and ask you: can the baptism of babies be supported by scripture?*

David: Before we get into that very big question, I'd like to add just a little about the history. Those who baptise babies freely admit that their primary argument for doing it comes from history rather than scripture. It goes back so far. It goes right back to the second century. But I'd just like to point out that it was also at that time that baptism did another unusual thing. Baptism was not only brought down to the birth of a baby. It was brought forward to the death of someone, and in the second century they had these two unusual developments – either baptising someone at birth or postponing it until death. And I think wrong thinking lay behind both these developments – the deathbed conversion idea was that you mustn't sin after baptism or it undid the whole thing, so you waited until the last moment of life so that you wouldn't sin again, and then you got baptised. That happened to Constantine in a later century.

So most 'baby baptisers' (and I much prefer that term to infant because an 'infant' covers a bit later as well), their main argument is from history. But it would be lovely if they could find an argument from scripture as well. That would immensely strengthen their case.

Interviewer: *I still want to go back to the second century. So you are saying that already – as early as in the second century – some foreign elements came to the church, and we cannot just take their examples to justify a particular position.*

David: No, there were a number of big changes during the period of what we call the Church Fathers – which was the earliest centuries. For example, the biggest change was from many bishops in one church to many churches to one bishop – and that was a huge change in structure. The church became more hierarchical and more like a pyramid structure, and there were many developments around that time which I feel are contrary to scripture, and infant baptism was one of them. Nevertheless, since then of course there has been a strong desire to find biblical basis for it as well, because for all Christians the Bible has a unique authority, and if you could find baby baptism somewhere in scripture, that would of course settle it for many.

So we must look at some of these scriptures that have been thought to be used. Now bear in mind that in those earliest times of the church they didn't have the full New Testament. They had the verbal teaching of the apostles' doctrine but it hadn't been written down yet. So the Bible of the early church was the Old Testament. That was the scripture as far as they were concerned, and of course whenever the New Testament apostles say 'according to scripture' they're referring to the Old Testament. And in the Old Testament the covenants that God made were with a whole nation, a whole people including the children, including the babies, because his covenants were made with Israel – not with Israelis but with Israel. They were not made with individual Jews but with the whole nation, which included babies, and so the covenant promises that God made in the Old Testament included babies, and that's true.

So the first argument from scripture that was used to justify baby baptism was: in the old covenant they circumcised babies; in the new covenant we baptise babies, and that there is an exact parallel between circumcision in the old and baptism in the new. That argument is still used, especially since there is one verse in the New Testament that uses the word 'circumcise' and the word 'baptise' together – Colossians 2:11. And on that one verse alone people have said: 'There, you see, baptism and circumcision are the same thing or much the same – one is the equivalent of the other.' Or the word usually used is 'parallel'. But, in fact, when you read that verse carefully, it is just the opposite. Paul is saying it is not circumcision of the flesh; that it is a circumcision inside, not outside the body. It is a circumcision of the heart that takes away the old flesh or the old nature; that that is the circumcision in Christ. That is what he is talking about, and amazingly, even in the Old Testament the prophets said, you've got circumcision of the body but you need circumcision of the heart. You need something cut out of your heart. So even the Old Testament talked about a different kind of circumcision and Colossians 2:11 talks about baptism in the context of that different kind of circumcision that is inward, not outward.

So that verse does not support a parallel. But one other point I need to make on that subject is that the biggest controversy in the New Testament was over circumcision, whether Gentile believers who were not Jews, coming to believe in a Jewish Messiah, should be circumcised. And

Paul fought tooth and nail against the idea that Gentile Christians needed to be circumcised. The reason he taught it was this. He said if you submit to that you are coming under, and putting yourself under, all the laws of Moses. You will have to keep the lot. If you become a Jew, you've got to keep the Jewish laws. And so he fought for our freedom from circumcision, and in the whole controversy – which was the subject of the first Jerusalem Council in Acts 15, and the subject of the whole of Paul's letter of Galatians – in the whole argument no-one thought of saying, 'We don't need circumcision because we have baptism.' Nobody thought of making a parallel between the two, which would have settled all the argument; which to me shows that they never thought of circumcision and baptism in the same light at all.

Now that was the argument for baby baptism from the Old Testament. But there have been many attempts to find justification in the New Testament. Now, all baby baptisers admit freely that there is no specific mention of baby baptism in the New Testament. There is no verse that says, 'This person and their baby were baptised.' Nor is there a single command in the New Testament that specifically says, 'Baptise your babies.' Now that is freely admitted. But it is what we call an argument from silence, which means to argue from what the Bible doesn't say, rather than what the Bible does say. And an argument from silence cuts both ways. It doesn't say baptise babies, but that doesn't imply that you don't do it. It doesn't say a baby was baptised, so how do you know a baby wasn't? You see, an argument from silence is a very tricky thing. You are better not to use it actually, so I don't use it. I argue from what the Bible does say.

So there are a number of ways in which baby baptisers quote certain New Testament scriptures and they are these. One is what Jesus said about children and what he did with children: 'Suffer the little children to come to me,' and he took them in his arms and blessed them; and, 'Unless you become as a little child, you can't enter the Kingdom of God.' I want to point out that 'child' is not 'baby'. He didn't say unless you become like a little baby, you can't enter the Kingdom. 'Except you become as a child' – and that's a big difference. A child is conscious, a child can make decisions, a child can do things; and when it says they brought children to Jesus and the disciples said, 'No, no; he hasn't time for children,' but Jesus said, 'Let the children come,' it doesn't say mothers carried babies, it says fathers brought children. Everybody thinks it was mothers who brought them, but it wasn't, it says 'fathers'. It is masculine. And these fathers brought children to Jesus for him to bless them, and Jesus blessed them. Jesus can bless children, and I asked him to bless my children. What he didn't do was baptise them, and he didn't say to the disciples, 'Baptise them, for of such is the Kingdom of God.' He blessed them – didn't baptise them; and they were children, not babies.

So to use those scriptures to support baby baptism is really going beyond what they say.

Interviewer: *I was about to say: what about when the Bible, in Acts, talks about especially households being baptised, and I understand they were quite large in those days. Weren't there any babies that were baptised? It says that the household was baptised.*

David: That's right. Well, there are two things to be said about that. There were five households that were baptised. I've baptised households.

Interviewer: *Really?*

David: The word 'household' does not mean 'family'. It's a different word; it's a much bigger word than our 'family'. We think of a family as father, mother, two children, a dog and the common cold – that's what we think of as a family. We have a very small notion of family anyway, but 'household' includes servants, slaves. It means literally everybody living under one roof, and when we fill in forms for the population census in Britain, the word 'household' is used. They want to know everybody in the household which doesn't mean necessarily relatives. It could be friends living or a lodger living, and in those days of course it included slaves. Now that is the first thing: it doesn't say families were baptised, it says households were.

Secondly, when you study it carefully you find that certain other things are said about the household as well as the fact that they were all baptised. For example, with the Philippian jailor, in Acts 16 (that's one example) – read that carefully and it says, 'Paul spoke the word to him and all the others in his house,' which means that Paul could preach the gospel to everybody in that household. When you study the other situation you find the same thing. Lydia, a businesswoman, may well not have been married at all, but she had staff. She had servants and in fact it happened in a prayer meeting – by the riverside – of women. It doesn't say children either. There was a prayer meeting and a group of women met to pray, and Paul baptised them at the riverside.

Interviewer: *Right there!*

David: Yes – you read it – and they were all praying, you see. So, again, in Cornelius, the same thing happens. Peter was preaching and the Holy Spirit came on all of them in his household. It says all that were listening were filled with the Spirit and then Peter said, 'How can we forbid water for these who have received the Spirit?'

Interviewer: *So only the ones who received of the Spirit were baptised?*

David: Right. So, when you study, it's only a superficial appeal that says, 'Households were baptised so we should.' Everybody under one roof heard the word, and this is to go back to something I said earlier – hearing the gospel and receiving it is necessary before baptism, and in the case of these households, that necessity was there. So they were conscious people, able to hear and receive what Paul was saying, and he then baptised them; and Peter did the same – after they had heard the message and received it. And in Cornelius's case, after they had received the Holy Spirit as well. So there were these preliminary conditions fulfilled before they baptised households. I have had a number of lovely baptisms of households where everybody in one house has become Christian and I have baptised the lot. So I believe in household baptisms. But there is another text in Acts that needs to be looked at. On the day of Pentecost, after Peter preached and the people were so feeling their guilt they said, 'What shall we do?' or, 'What must we do?' Peter said, 'Repent and be baptised each one of you for the forgiveness of sins and you will receive the Holy Spirit because the promise is to you and to your children.' Now that has been picked up by many baby baptisers and they said, 'There we are: *and to your children.*' Well, they don't quote the rest of the verse unfortunately. It immediately adds, 'as many as the Lord calls.' So your children – and by the way, the promise isn't baptism, it is *baptism in the Holy Spirit* that is the promise – and that promise of receiving the Holy Spirit is 'to you and to your children, as many as the Lord calls.' So they have to be children who hear the call, and not only that, but Peter has already said, 'Whoever calls on the name of the Lord will be saved.' Therefore, the word 'children' there must be qualified by two calls: as many as the Lord calls; and as many as call on him. Now, all your children whom the Lord calls and who call on him will be saved and receive the promise of the Holy Spirit.

Once again, when you don't just quote a verse out of context, but look into it carefully, it doesn't actually say what people want it to say.

So we've got the Old Testament covenant idea that babies are included – they *were* included. Abraham and his children and his babies, they were all included. Babies were circumcised. But the new covenant, which is what we are under, in the New Testament, is intensely individualistic. That comes as a surprise to some people. The old covenants were corporate. They were to a nation, to everybody within it. The new covenant is very definitely addressed to individuals.

In Jeremiah 31, where it is first announced, it says, 'And each will know me first hand.' Each! And throughout the New Testament, the teaching of the gospel, the preaching of the gospel is addressed to individuals, not families. I have already quoted one. Listen to this. When they said, 'Peter, what shall we do?' – he said, 'Repent and be baptised each one of you....' That is the appeal of the gospel. On the Day of Judgment we can answer for no-one but ourselves – not our family, not our children, not our parents. On the Day of Judgment, we stand before God by ourselves, and in the Day of Salvation, we stand for ourselves. Each one is responsible for their relationship to God. It is a very individual thing, and all evangelists appeal to individuals – each one to repent and believe. This is the emphasis right through the new covenant. The new covenant is not made with families, it is not made with nations. It is made with each creature that God has made, and each person must respond for themselves and no-one else. You can't make your children Christian. I wish you could. You can't do it. They must come to Christ for themselves. You can't in fact be responsible for anyone else before God. You can do everything you can to help someone to be saved, but I can't decide that someone else should be saved, even my own children.

Interviewer: *But I've heard many times people who teach infant baptism say that it is possible for a baby to believe – and, in a sense, who is to say that a baby couldn't believe?*

So is there any scriptural proof that a baby couldn't believe?

David: It is interesting that Martin Luther defended infant baptism by saying, 'Who can prove that a baby can't believe?' Well, I just want to answer that by saying, 'Who can prove a baby can?' But in the New Testament, believing is not an instinctive trust. It is a mental response as well as the response of the heart and will. It is a response to a message. It is a response to the gospel. And therefore, in Romans 10, Paul makes it quite clear, 'How shall they hear without a preacher; how will they believe if they don't hear?'

In other words, New Testament faith is not an instinctive trust without content. It is the response to a message – and therefore, how can a baby believe without hearing? It is impossible. And of course, that will have an effect on our evangelism.

Interviewer: *So you need to hear to believe, and I want to talk about this evangelism. But before that, there's one more thing. We were talking a lot about the Holy Spirit, the receiving of the Holy Spirit, the baptism of the Holy Spirit. And sometimes I have heard many people say that, when we are baptised we have also been baptised in the Holy Spirit, we receive the Holy Spirit. Doesn't the Bible link baptism and the Holy Spirit and receiving of the Holy Spirit?*

David: You know, in all these attempts to justify baby baptism from scripture, two things that are distinctly different are being confused: circumcision and baptism are being confused; babies and children are being confused; households and families are being confused. Now this confusion is a very common one, and it is to believe that baptism in water and baptism in the Spirit are one and the same thing. They are quite different things in the New Testament. They never happen at the same moment. They either happen near together or even far apart, and one can happen before the other or the other before the one. But they are always distinct. It was for Jesus himself. He went down into the Jordan and was baptised in water and then it says he came up out of the water and prayed and the Holy Spirit came like a dove on him. And in every other case, baptism in water and baptism in the Holy Spirit are quite distinct things. They may happen quite close together, one after the other or one before the other, or they may happen months apart.

In Acts 8, the people of Samaria repented, believed, were baptised in water and rejoiced, and the whole city was full of joy. A modern evangelist would be thrilled to bits and say, 'My work is finished.' They didn't in those days! The apostles came rushing down from Jerusalem – because none of them had received the Holy Spirit. There was quite a gap between. The same thing happened in Ephesus, in Acts 19. They had been baptised in water. Paul found they had only been baptised in John's water as it were, and not in the name of Jesus, so he then baptised them in the name of Jesus, and then he laid hands on them and prayed and the Holy Spirit came on them.

So here are two baptisms that every Christian needs: one in water; one in Spirit. I believe John 3:5 refers to these two baptisms. This is a literal translation – 'Unless a man is born again out of water...' – the word 'out' is rarely quoted – 'and out of Spirit....' Well, to be born out of water and out of Spirit, you need to be plunged into water and into Spirit.

Do you know, from the very beginning of the Gospels, all four Gospels distinguished between baptism in water and baptism in Spirit.

All four Gospels quote John as saying, 'I'll baptise you in water, but there's somebody coming after me who'll baptise you in the Spirit.' And, in fact, a human being can baptise me in water, but only Jesus himself can baptise me in the Holy Spirit, so I have to go to two different people for the two things. So it is there in the very beginning of each

Gospel – John said, 'I can only baptise you in water.' But you'll need something more than that.

And one of the reasons why he said it is this: Baptism in water essentially deals with your *past*. It doesn't change your *future*. It washes away the past, it buries the past, it gives you a clean start. There is another scripture, 1 Peter 3, where Peter says, 'Baptism now saves you, not by washing dirt from your body....'

Interviewer: *So it means to actually physically wash you. Do you think that means that?*

David: Yes, he's talking about baptism in water, and he says baptism now saves you, not by washing dirt from your body but by an appeal to God for a clean conscience. In other words, God wants us to start the Christian life clean – with a clean conscience; nothing on our conscience – and he does that in baptism, so while the body is immersed in water, God is washing the inside and cleansing us. So there we are. Now how did I get on to that?

Interviewer: *No, it was good that you mentioned that. I want to now go on to a subject like evangelism. But when I think about evangelism of course I think about the Great Commission, and when I think about the Great Commission, I suddenly think: weren't the disciples commanded to baptise first and then teach? Isn't that an example of Jesus basically giving a possibility of baptising infants before and teaching them later?*

David: Let's look a bit more closely. He didn't say baptise them and preach.

Interviewer: *That's right.*

David: And there's a big difference between preaching and teaching in the New Testament. Preaching is sharing the gospel; teaching is helping people to live the Christian life, and it doesn't say 'baptising them and then preaching the gospel to them' – it says, 'baptising them and teaching them how to do all the things I've told you.' Because, after baptism, we need instruction in how to live the Christian life. That is not about preaching the gospel. Take Mark's Gospel at the end: preach the gospel to every creature. He who believes and is baptised will be saved. That's the order. The preaching comes before baptism. The teaching comes after, and teaching is not preaching. How did we get on to that?

Interviewer: *It's evangelism.*

David: Right – let's talk about that.

Interviewer: *What are the effects of this teaching of yours and also the infant baptism? What are the effects of all this in evangelism?*

David: Well, the first thing I want to say is that baptism has been shifted from a context of evangelism, which it has in the New Testament, to the context of church membership, and it is seen today, not so much as a response to the gospel as an admission to the church. Do you see what I mean?

Interviewer: *Yes.*

David: In the New Testament, its context is evangelism. Now it has become a church membership issue. I believe we need to put it back into evangelism. First, for the very simple reason that this is the Bible way of accepting the gospel, and since we have moved it into church membership we are left with a vacuum in evangelism. What do we tell people to do? You see? And we have thought up a host of things, most of which only began in America in nineteenth-century revivalism like: 'Put your hand up, come to the front, sign a decision card.' None of these things you find in the New Testament. They are all substitutes for baptism. In the New Testament, when you preached the gospel as Peter did on the Day of Pentecost and people said, 'What must we do about it?' – he said, 'Repent and be baptised.' I long to hear a modern evangelist quote that verse: Acts 2:38. 'Repent and be baptised each one of you for the forgiveness of sins and you will receive the Holy Spirit.'

That was the appeal and it was a very definite appeal. They knew exactly what they had to do, and notice that they had to prove repentance before they could be baptised. You know, people think repentance is just saying 'sorry'– you know the 'sinner's prayer' – 'Lord, I'm sorry for all my sins.' That is not repentance! Nothing like repentance. Here is a verse that I've never heard anyone preach on. It's a verse that begins, 'I was not disobedient to the heavenly vision'. Now I am sure you have heard that verse; every preacher has used it. None of them quote the whole thing. Paul says, 'I was not disobedient to the heavenly vision so I....' Did what? You know, I shouldn't test you, I've yet to meet a Christian who can tell me the rest of the verse. He says, 'So I preached repentance to the Gentiles that they should turn to God and prove their repentance by their deeds.'

Interviewer: *That's right.*

David: And somebody's going to say that is salvation by works. Nothing of the kind! Prove their repentance by their deeds. In other words, I tell people I don't baptise someone now on profession of faith but on proof of repentance, and this is a shock to many people. They have never had to prove their repentance by their deeds. But, you see, an evangelism that said that would be totally different. But I have never heard an evangelist use that passage Acts 2:38–39. Never! And yet that is what the apostle said. We call it 'the Peter package' – and a few evangelists I do know actually are now using the Peter package and are saying, 'Repent and be baptised every one of you for the forgiveness of sins.' That is the biblical way of responding to the gospel when you hear it, and we think up so many other different ways because we've moved baptism to church membership, out of evangelism. But we should follow Jesus' orders. He said, 'Go and make disciples of all nations, baptising them and then teaching them how to do all that I've told you.' You see?

But there is another way in which it is affecting evangelism. When you are trying to evangelise in a nation that has had a State Church, in which everybody has been baptised as babies, you really are up against something, because you are up against the feeling: 'Oh! But I was baptised as a baby. I'm alright. I'm a Christian. I'm going to heaven. I'm part of the church. How dare you come and tell me I'm a sinner and need salvation.' There is an inbuilt immunisation against the gospel and it really is difficult. It is easier in a completely pagan situation because they know they are not Christians. They know they are sinners. They know they are bad. So it does make evangelism very very difficult, and indeed it makes it a bit of a contradiction. You are telling people that they are not what they thought they were. You are saying, 'You're not Christians yet, so accept Christ.'

'But I am a Christian; I've been baptised!'

Well I think we must move on.

Interviewer: *Yes. Do you think that a person who is not baptised as a believer is missing something?*

David: Yes. I know many Christians who don't take the Lord's Supper – they don't eat bread and drink wine as Jesus told us to – mainly in the Salvation Army. But there are other Christians I know who never take that. And if someone asks me, 'Are they missing something?' I say, 'Of course they are. Jesus would not command us to do something that is unnecessary and it was he who commanded us to take bread and wine.' And it was he who commanded us to be immersed in water. I cannot think that Jesus was just doing it as a kind of optional extra. When Jesus tells me to do something, I do it. And if I don't do it, I'm going to miss something.

Now I think what may be behind the question is revealed when people then say, 'Are you telling me I won't go to heaven unless I am baptised? Are you telling me I can't be saved without baptism?' You see, the trouble is when people think of the word 'saved' they immediately think of the next life – heaven and hell. Jesus didn't come to save us from hell, that is a bonus thrown in. It says, 'Call him Jesus because he will save his people from their sins.' Unfortunately, most people want to be saved from hell, not their sins. But baptism is to help us to be saved from our sins, by giving us a clean conscience to begin with; and if people want to be saved from their sins, *all* of them, then they need baptism. But you see, when it's twisted to say, 'Do you mean I won't go to heaven until I'm baptised?' you've put the question into the wrong context. But yes.

Interviewer: *We've talked about doctrinal issues, we've talked about churches, we've talked about different rites and things, but what must all this have to do with Jesus? Can you finish with this question?*

David: Well, we wouldn't even discuss it if it wasn't for Jesus. It was Jesus who commanded it, and he not only gave us a command to do it – and if I claim to be a follower of Jesus and don't do what he commands, I'm a living contradiction – but he also gave us an example, and the one person who didn't need to be baptised was Jesus. The one person who didn't need to be cleaned up was Jesus. And John the Baptist said to his cousin Jesus: 'You, coming to me for baptism? I should be baptised by you' – which says the man who baptised Jesus himself had not been baptised himself. Isn't that amazing? Because it is not the person who baptises you that matters, it is the baptism. But for Jesus it was not a cleansing. What was it? He said: 'It is right for us to do what is right' and, therefore, he gave us an example, and if anybody who claims to follow Jesus says, 'I don't need it', I just don't know how they can say that. If he needed it to do what was right, I do too. And I have followed Jesus and been baptised in the way that I believe he intended, as clearly taught in the New Testament.

Interviewer: *Thank you so much, Mr Pawson. I think those words were a good way to finish the discussion. I believe your thorough teaching has been very helpful for many. Thank you so much for being with us and being here in Finland as a blessing.*

David: Thank you.

ABOUT DAVID PAWSON

A speaker and author with uncompromising faithfulness to the Holy Scriptures, David brings clarity and a message of urgency to Christians to uncover hidden treasures in God's Word.

Born in England in 1930, David began his career with a degree in Agriculture from Durham University. When God intervened and called him to become a Minister, he completed an MA in Theology at Cambridge University and served as a Chaplain in the Royal Air Force for three years. He moved on to pastor several churches, including the Millmead Centre in Guildford, which became a model for many UK church leaders. In 1979, the Lord led him into an international ministry. His current itinerant ministry is predominantly to church leaders. David and his wife Enid currently reside in the county of Hampshire in the UK.

Over the years, he has written a large number of books, booklets, and daily reading notes. His extensive and very accessible overviews of the books of the Bible have been published and recorded in *Unlocking the Bible*. Millions of copies of his teachings have been distributed in more than 120 countries, providing a solid biblical foundation.

He is reputed to be the "most influential Western preacher in China" through the broadcast of his best-selling *Unlocking the Bible* series into every Chinese province by Good TV. In the UK, David's teachings are often broadcast on Revelation TV.

Countless believers worldwide have also benefited from his generous decision in 2011 to make available his extensive audio video teaching library free of charge at www.davidpawson.org and we have recently uploaded all of David's video to a dedicated channel on www.youtube.com

THE EXPLAINING SERIES
BIBLICAL TRUTHS SIMPLY EXPLAINED

If you have been blessed reading this book, there are more available in the series. Please register to download more booklets for free by visiting
www.explainingbiblicaltruth.global

Other booklets in the *Explaining* series will include:
The Amazing Story of Jesus
The Resurrection: *The Heart of Christianity*
Studying the Bible
Being Anointed and Filled with the Holy Spirit
New Testament Baptism
How to study a book of the Bible: Jude
The Key Steps to Becoming a Christian
What the Bible says about Money
What the Bible says about Work
Grace – *Undeserved Favour, Irresistible Force or Unconditional Forgiveness?*
Eternally secure? – *What the Bible says about being saved*
De-Greecing the Church – The impact of Greek thinking on Christian beliefs
Three texts often taken out of context:
Expounding the truth and exposing error
The Trinity
The Truth about Christmas

They will also be avaiable to purchase as print copies from:
Amazon or **www.thebookdepository.com**

UNLOCKING THE BIBLE

A unique overview of both the Old and New Testaments, from internationally acclaimed evangelical speaker and author David Pawson. *Unlocking the Bible* opens up the Word of God in a fresh and powerful way. Avoiding the small detail of verse by verse studies, it sets out the epic story of God and his people in Israel. The culture, historical background and people are introduced and the teaching applied to the modern world. Eight volumes have been brought into one compact and easy to use guide to cover both the Old and New Testaments in one massive omnibus edition. *The Old Testament: The Maker's Instructions* (The five books of law); *A Land and A Kingdom* (Joshua, Judges, Ruth, 1&2 Samuel, 1&2 Kings); *Poems of Worship and Wisdom* (Psalms, Song of Solomon, Proverbs, Ecclesiastes, Job); *Decline and Fall of an Empire* (Isaiah, Jeremiah and other prophets); *The Struggle to Survive* (Chronicles and prophets of exile); *The New Testament: The Hinge of History* (Mathew, Mark, Luke, John and Acts); *The Thirteenth Apostle* (Paul and his letters); *Through Suffering to Glory* (Hebrews, the letters of James, Peter and Jude, the Book of Revelation). Already an international bestseller.

JESUS: THE SEVEN WONDERS OF HISTORY

This book is the result of a lifetime of telling 'the greatest story ever told' around the world. David re-told it to many hundreds of young people in Kansas City, USA, who heard it with uninhibited enthusiasm, 'tweeting' on the internet about 'this cute old English gentleman' even while he was speaking.

Taking the middle section of the Apostles' Creed as a framework, David explains the fundamental facts about Jesus on which the Christian faith is based in a fresh and stimulating way. Both old and new Christians will benefit from this 'back to basics' call and find themselves falling in love with their Lord all over again.

OTHER TEACHINGS
BY DAVID PAWSON

For the most up to date list of David's Books go to: **www.davidpawsonbooks.com**

To purchase David's Teachings go to: **www.davidpawson.com**

www.ingramcontent.com/pod-product-compliance
Lightning Source LLC
Chambersburg PA
CBHW071040080526
44587CB00015B/2705